A MESSAGE FOR OUR TIME

A MESSAGE FOR OUR TIME—

*on tolerance, public service, and
the pursuit of peace*

A Compilation of Speeches

of

His Holiness Mirza Masroor Ahmad

*Imam and the Head of the Worldwide Ahmadiyya Muslim Jama'at,
Fifth Successor to the Promised Messiah*[as]*, may Allah the Almighty be his Helper*

ISLAM INTERNATIONAL PUBLICATIONS LTD.

A Message for Our Time—
on tolerance, public service, and the pursuit of peace

A Compilation of Keynote Addresses
delivered by
His Holiness Mirza Masroor Ahmad
Head of the Worldwide Ahmadiyya Muslim Community
Fifth Successor to the Promised Messiah[as]
During his 2018 Americas Tour

First Published in the UK, 2019

© Islam International Publications Ltd.

Published by

Islam International Publications Ltd
Unit 3, Bourne Mill Business Park,
Guildford Road, Farnham, Surrey UK, GU9 9PS

For further information please visit: www.alislam.org

ISBN: 978-1-84880-325-1
10 9 8 7 6 5 4 3 2 1

CONTENTS

Hazrat Mirza Masroor Ahmad
Khalifatul-Masih V[aba]

ABOUT THE AUTHOR

His Holiness, Mirza Masroor Ahmad, Khalifatul-Masih V[aba], is the supreme head of the worldwide Ahmadiyya Muslim Community. He is the Fifth Khalifah of the Promised Messiah and Reformer, Hazrat Mirza Ghulam Ahmad[as] of Qadian.

His Holiness was born on September 15, 1950 in Rabwah, Pakistan to the late Mirza Mansoor Ahmad and the late Nasirah Begum Ahmad. Upon completing his Masters Degree in Agricultural Economics in 1977 from the Agriculture University in Faisalabad, Pakistan, he formally dedicated his life to the service of Islam. He was sent to Ghana in 1977 where, for several years, he served as a principal of various Ahmadiyya Muslim schools.

Later, when His Holiness returned to Pakistan, he served in various capacities at the Headquarters of the Ahmadiyya Muslim Community in Rabwah.

Elected to the lifelong position of Khalifah (Caliph) of the Ahmadiyya Muslim Community on 22nd April 2003, His Holiness serves as the worldwide spiritual and administrative head of an international religious organization with tens of millions of members spread across more than 200 countries.

Since being elected Khalifah, His Holiness has led a worldwide campaign to convey the peaceful message of Islam, through all forms of print and digital media. Under his leadership, national branches of the Ahmadiyya Muslim Community have launched campaigns that reflect the true and peaceful teachings of Islam. Ahmadi Muslims the world over are engaged in grassroots efforts to distribute millions of 'peace' leaflets to Muslims and non-Muslims alike, host interfaith and peace symposia and organize exhibitions of the Holy Qur'an to present its true and noble message. These campaigns have received worldwide media coverage and demonstrate that Islam champions peace, loyalty to one's country of residence and service to humanity.

In 2004, His Holiness launched the annual National Peace Symposium in which guests from all walks of life come together to exchange ideas on the promotion of peace and harmony. Each year, the symposium attracts many serving ministers, parliamentarians, politicians, religious leaders and other dignitaries.

His Holiness has travelled globally to promote and facilitate service to humanity. Under the leadership of His Holiness, the Ahmadiyya Muslim Community has built a number of schools and hospitals that provide excellent education and healthcare in remote parts of the world.

His Holiness strives to establish peace at every level of society. He constantly advises members of the Ahmadiyya Muslim Community to carry out a 'jihad' (or struggle) of the self to strive to reform individually, which is the true and biggest form of 'jihad,' so that every Ahmadi Muslim can first establish peace on an individual level, and then be enabled to also help others find peace.

At an individual and collective level, on local, national and international platforms, His Holiness is striving to advise all others of the practical means of establishing peace, based on the true teachings of Islam.

His Holiness, Mirza Masroor Ahmad[aba] currently resides in London, England. As spiritual leader of Ahmadi Muslims all over the world, he vigorously champions the cause of Islam through a refreshing message of peace and compassion.

INTRODUCTION

We are passing through a crucial time in history where the world is increasingly segregated and growing anxious of one another. Global strife and catastrophe seem likely, if not inevitable, and yet a solution for peace and reconciliation exists and can be found in practice. This book is a collection of the four lectures that His Holiness, Mirza Masroor Ahmad, the head of the worldwide Ahmadiyya Muslim Community, delivered during his 2018 tour of North and Central America.

During this visit, His Holiness delivered luminary speeches at the inaugurations of mosques in Philadelphia, Baltimore, and Virginia. He also gave a historic address in Guatemala, launching the Nasir Hospital, a project steered by the efforts of Humanity First.

His Holiness explains how the establishment of mosques and hospitals helps dispel the wrongful misconceptions held about Islam and its founder, Prophet Muhammad, may peace and blessings of Allah be upon him. The true spirit of worship and the real purpose of mosques went missing for centuries, but is being revived by Hazrat Mirza Ghulam Ahmad, the Promised Messiah[as] and his Community today. With the world heading to the brink of disaster, His Holiness Mirza Masroor Ahmad makes a call for lasting peace through the establishment of mutual religious tolerance and human compassion. By uniting in prayers to God Almighty and by discharging our responsibilities to our fellow neighbours, we are able to fulfil our true purpose in life. In doing so, we try our best to bring about the peaceful changes needed in the world today.

Al-Haaj Munir-ud-Din Shams
Additional Wakilut-Tasneef
London
January 2019

SPEECHES

A BEACON OF PEACE

Hazrat Mirza Masroor Ahmad, Khalifatul-Masih V[aba] Receives the Key to the City
of Philadelphia from Honourable James Kenney, Mayor of Philadelphia

Hazrat Mirza Masroor Ahmad, Khalifatul-Masih V[aba] Leads Guests of the Baitul-Aafiyat Reception in Silent Prayers. Special Guests Seated Include Honourable James Kenney (Mayor of Philadelphia), Honourable Dwight Evans (U.S. Congressman), Honourable Sharif Street (Member, Pennsylvania State Senate) and Professor Istvan Varkonyi (Temple University)

Preface

On the evening of 19th October 2018, the Head of the Worldwide Ahmadiyya Muslim Community, the Fifth Khalifah, His Holiness Hazrat Mirza Masroor Ahmad[aba], delivered the keynote address at a special reception held to mark the inauguration of the 'Baitul-Aafiyat' (House of Security) Mosque in Philadelphia, USA. The mosque, which is the first purpose-built mosque in Philadelphia, was officially opened earlier in the day when His Holiness delivered his weekly Friday Sermon. Over 175 dignitaries and guests attended the evening reception held in the new mosque. The event concluded with a silent prayer led by His Holiness. Later, His Holiness personally met with many of the guests who attended the reception. Prior to the reception, the Mayor of Philadelphia, James Kenny and Congressman Dwight Evans were able to have a personal audience with His Holiness. His Holiness also met members of the assembled media and answered questions about the objectives of the new mosque and other related issues.

A BEACON OF PEACE

After reciting tashahhud, ta'awwuz and bismillaah,[1] *Hazrat Mirza Masroor Ahmad*[aba]*, the Head of the Worldwide Ahmadiyya Muslim Community, said:*

---◦⤙⟡⤚◦---

All distinguished guests, *Assalaamo alaikum wa Rahmatullaahe wa Barakaatohu*—peace and blessings of Allah be upon you all.

First of all, I would like to thank all of our guests who have graciously accepted our invitation and joined us at this special and joyous occasion, where we are inaugurating our new mosque in this city.

It is a fact of life that human beings are such creatures who cannot survive without social interaction and without developing

---

1 This is the traditional Islamic opening in Arabic for an address. For the benefit of readers, we have presented its translation in the Glossary. [Publisher]

mutual relations with other people. Irrespective of differences of race, religion or social background, we are united as human beings and so it is vital that we interact with other people, rather than isolating ourselves or only mingling with members of our own particular community.

In all respects, dialogue is crucial to breaking down barriers and increasing mutual understanding and knowledge. For the advancement and evolution of society, and to foster an atmosphere of peace and togetherness, respectful discourse and discussion between people and amongst different communities is vital. Therefore, I hold all of you in great esteem for taking time out of your busy lives to join us here today. Regardless of the fact that most of you are not Muslims, you have accepted our invitation and joined us at this purely religious event, where a mosque is being opened. Thus, I cannot proceed further without praising your high levels of tolerance and respect.

Where your participation is a sign of your desire to strengthen your personal ties with members of our community, it also symbolises your eagerness to gain a richer understanding of our religion. It illustrates that you are people who are unwilling to blindly accept hearsay or second-hand information.

In today's era, where so many reports are inaccurate, your search for the truth about Islam can only be commended. Rather than accepting what the media says about Muslims or what anti-Islamic powers try to portray, you have come to see for yourselves what Islam means and represents. For this, I applaud you and offer my sincere thanks.

You may well be aware that the slogan or motto of the Ahmadiyya Muslim Community is, 'Love for All, Hatred for

None'. This motto is nothing new, or something we have suddenly fashioned; rather, this slogan is based on the teachings of
Islam's Holy Book, the Holy Quran, and the teachings given to us
by the Founder of Islam, the Holy Prophet Muhammad[sas]. From
the outset, Islam has taught that mutual respect and tolerance are
basic human values. For example, in chapter 6, verse 109, the Holy
Quran declares that Muslims should not even speak against the
idols of non-religious people because it could provoke them to
speak against Allah the Almighty. Thus, to ensure that tensions
are not inflamed and to protect society from a cycle of hate and
hostility, Muslims have been instructed to show restraint and
patience at all times.

Whilst it is frequently alleged that Muslims do not respect
other religions or their religious figures, nothing could be further from the truth. In fact, based upon the teachings of the Holy
Quran, Muslims believe that prophets of God were sent to all
nations in order to guide and reform the people of those regions.
We firmly believe in the truth of all the prophets and believe they
were sent to draw mankind towards God Almighty and to teach
morality and to establish universal human values, such as freedom
of conscience, justice and human sympathy. Given this, how could
it be possible for us to disrespect or dishonour other religions, or
their followers?

Hence, we Ahmadi Muslims are sincere in our claim that we
do not hate anyone. Moreover, we hold genuine love for all people
and are ever-ready to extend a hand of friendship to others. Just
to give one small example, last year when a local Jewish cemetery
was attacked here in Philadelphia and their gravestones were dese-
crated, the local members of the Ahmadiyya Muslim Community

immediately went to offer their support to the Jewish community and to stand in solidarity with them after that despicable crime. We seek no reward or gratitude for such things, because we are merely following what our religion has taught us, which is to stand shoulder to shoulder with the people of other faiths and beliefs in their times of need or distress. We champion the right of all people to live their lives, free from discrimination or prejudice.

Anyone who is willing to look at Islamic history, objectively and honestly, will see that universal freedom of belief has always been a core tenet of Islam. Indeed, a great manifestation of such pluralism and broad-mindedness was the government that was formed in the Arabian city of Madinah, where the Holy Prophet Muhammad[sas] migrated to, along with many of his followers, after facing years of persecution in Makkah. Alongside the leaders of other religions and communities, the Prophet of Islam[sas] established a covenant that served as the basis for governance in that diverse city. It ensured that all members of society were able to live in peace, free from oppression, and were free to practice their religion or beliefs. Furthermore, according to the customs of the time, each community was bound by their own religious laws or tribal customs. Thus, Muslims followed laws based upon the Islamic **Shariah**, Jewish people followed laws based upon the Torah and other communities followed laws according to their own customs and beliefs.

At the same time, all people, no matter their faith, had a responsibility to uphold the peace of the state and to treat others with respect. The treaty fostered peace and ensured that a tolerant society prevailed. Thus, more than 1400 years ago, a multicultural melting-pot of a society was successfully managed and administered in Madinah. I am not suggesting that in today's world there should be a myriad of different laws that exist for different communities living in the same society; rather, my point is simply that our leading priority should always be to establish peace in society, by upholding universal human values and by promoting morality and justice at all levels of society. To explain further, the Holy Quran and the Prophet of Islam^{sas} have made it categorically clear that there should be no form of compulsion in matters of religion. Every individual should have the right to choose whatever path he or she wishes to walk upon. Belief is, and should always remain, a matter for one's heart and one's mind.

At the same time, Islam teaches that, irrespective of differences of religion or belief, every citizen has a duty to remain peaceful and to ensure that he or she does not take any action that threatens the well-being of society. Islam states that all people should be law-abiding and loyal citizens of the state and work towards its progress and development. Hence, if any of you harbour reservations about this new mosque and fear it will be used by Muslims to plot and scheme against the rest of society or to incite hatred, let me reassure you that there is no need for any such anxiety or concern. Rest assured that from this building, only a message of love, affection, and brotherhood will shine forth.

In this regard, I would like to briefly explain what the purposes of a mosque are. The primary objective of a mosque is to enable Muslims to join together, with a spirit of mutual love and unity, to worship the One God, in the way He has taught. At the same time, the second core objective of a mosque is to be a centre for serving mankind. Every worshipper has a profound responsibility to fulfil the rights of all other members of society. Consequently, a true mosque is both a symbol and manifestation of compassion, benevolence and unity. The history of the Ahmadiyya Muslim Community testifies to the fact that wherever in the world we open mosques, our members who worship there increase their standards of love, sympathy and loyalty towards their fellow citizens. If our mosques serve to incite Ahmadi Muslims, it is not towards terrorism or extremism, it is only towards serving humanity and opening our hearts to our fellow beings. Our mosques increase our determination to spread peace and to cultivate bonds of brotherhood and mutual affection with people from all walks of life and to eliminate all forms of hatred, bigotry and division from society.

This city is known as the 'City of Brotherly Love' and certainly, our new mosque is a sign, and indeed a commitment from us, pledging to intensify our efforts to spread love, brotherhood and goodwill here and beyond. Whilst it is easy to make such claims, our history proves that our words are not shallow, but have real substance. At all times, we strive to practice what we preach. Thus, I am entirely confident that the local community will soon come to appreciate that this mosque, which has been named 'Baitul-Aafiyat', and literally means a 'House of Security', is a true source of peace for the entire society.

Furthermore, I would like to make it crystal clear that our commitment to peace and our vow to serve humanity is due entirely to our faith and our religious teachings. The Founder of the Ahmadiyya Muslim Community, who we believe to be the Promised Messiah and Imam Mahdi (Guided One), openly proclaimed that he was the Messiah of Muhammad[sas] and that he would follow in the peaceful footsteps of the Messiah who

followed Moses[as]. And he declared that he had been sent by God
Almighty with two outstanding purposes.

Firstly, he was sent to bring mankind back towards its Creator
and to draw the attention of people towards fulfilling His rights.
Secondly, he came to urge humanity to respect human values and
to fulfil the rights of one another. Hence, it is incumbent upon
all Ahmadi Muslims, who have accepted the Promised Messiah
and Imam Mahdi, to seek every opportunity to become closer
to God Almighty and to serve mankind. This is what we have
been repeatedly taught by the Holy Quran and the Holy Prophet
Muhammad[sas]. In chapter 4, verse 37, the Holy Quran states:

> And worship Allah and associate naught with Him, and
> *show* kindness to parents, and to kindred, and orphans,
> and the needy, and to the neighbour who is a kinsman and
> the neighbour who is a stranger, and the companion by
> *your* side, and the wayfarer, and those whom your right
> hands possess. Surely, Allah loves not the arrogant *and* the
> boastful.

This single verse of the Quran is a magnificent charter of morality
and human rights. It is a golden pathway to peace and a means to
brotherly love. In this verse, apart from His worship, Allah the
Almighty commands Muslims to treat their parents and relatives
with love and affection. He commands them to support and comfort the most vulnerable members of society, such as orphans or
those deprived in any way. Thereafter, special mention is made to
fulfilling the rights of one's neighbours. Muslims are taught to

love and protect their neighbours and to be ever ready to help them in their times of need.

Furthermore, I should clarify that the definition of a 'neighbour' in Islam is extremely vast. It not only includes people who live nearby, but also includes people who live further afield, a person's travel companions, work colleagues, subordinates and many others besides. In effect, the Holy Quran has declared that all the people living in a Muslim's town or city are their neighbours. The Holy Prophet of Islam[sas] also repeatedly instructed Muslims to fulfil the rights of their neighbours. Indeed, he said Allah the Almighty had emphasised the importance of discharging the rights of one's neighbours so fervently to him that he began to think that perhaps they would be included amongst a person's rightful inheritors. Consequently, if we have built a mosque here in Philadelphia, and if we have established a community of Ahmadi Muslims, we have done so with the intention of increasing the peace and prosperity of this city and serving its people.

Now that this mosque is open, the local Ahmadi Muslims will consider all people in this city as their neighbours and recognise that they have many rights over them and will strive to fulfil them to the best of their abilities. Whenever any of you stand in need of help, we pledge to be there to aid and assist, in whatever way we can.

In times of grief and despair, we will always be there to wipe away the tears of our neighbours and to support and comfort them.

Thus, I am sure that you will see for yourselves that where this new mosque is an added physical attraction and landmark in this city, even more significantly, it will spiritually enhance and beautify the society by spreading love and kindness across the city and far beyond. It will prove a beacon of light and hope to all peace-loving people, irrespective of their caste, creed, or colour.

With these words, I hope and pray that all people in this city, no matter who they are, or what they believe in, join together and work towards the common good and seek to foster an atmosphere of true and long-lasting peace.

It is said that Philadelphia was the first colonial city which permitted freedom of religion and freedom of worship in this country. Furthermore, it is the historic city where the Declaration of Independence was signed. Hence, this city has a rich and proud history and it is my prayer that its people are able to build upon their distinguished past and that these great traditions remain a hallmark of your future.

I pray that this city forever remains a beacon of freedom of belief and that the people of this city each play their role in advancing peace, not only in this city but throughout the United States and indeed, across the world. Even though our membership here remains quite small, I assure you that the Ahmadiyya Muslim Community will always stand ready to support such noble efforts and to offer any help required.

May Allah the Almighty enable for true peace to prevail in all cities and nations.

At the end, I wish to express my sincere thanks to all of you for joining us here today.

May Allah bless you all.

Thank you very much.

MOSQUES—
CENTRES OF LOVE & PEACE

INAUGURATION OF THE BAITUS-SAMAD MOSQUE
BALTIMORE, MARYLAND, USA
OCTOBER 20, 2018

Hazrat Mirza Masroor Ahmad, Khalifatul-Masih V[aba] Meets with Honourable Ben Cardin, U.S. Senator

Hazrat Mirza Masroor Ahmad, Khalifatul-Masih V[aba] Receives a Special Recognition from the Governor of Maryland, Larry Hogan, Presented by Honourable John Wobensmith (Secretary of State, Maryland)

Preface

On 20th October 2018, the Head of the Worldwide Ahmadiyya Muslim Community, the Fifth Khalifah, His Holiness Hazrat Mirza Masroor Ahmad[aba] inaugurated the Baitus-Samad Mosque in Baltimore, USA before delivering the keynote address at a special reception held to mark its opening. Upon arriving in Baltimore, His Holiness officially inaugurated the mosque by unveiling a commemorative plaque and offering a silent prayer in thanks to God Almighty. Thereafter, His Holiness led the *Zuhr* and *Asr* prayers at the mosque and inspected the new premises. In the evening, 500 people attended a special reception held at the Hilton Hotel, Baltimore, including 320 dignitaries and guests. His Holiness privately met with a range of dignitaries, including Honourable Ben Cardin and Honourable Catherine Pugh, Mayor of Baltimore. His Holiness also answered questions during a press conference with the assembled media. A range of dignitaries also addressed the audience, including United States Senator Ben Cardin and Honourable John Wobensmith, Secretary of State of Maryland.

MOSQUES—
CENTRES OF LOVE & PEAᴄ

Hazrat Mirza Masroor Ahmad, Khalifatul Masih V ᵃᵇᵃ, the Head of the Worldwide Ahmadiyya Muslim Community, said:

———◦⸲⨯◈⨯⸲◦———

Bismillaahir-Rahmaanir-Raheem—In the Name of Allah, the Gracious, Ever Merciful.

All distinguished guests, *Assalaamo alaikum wa Rahmatullaahe wa Barakaatohu*—peace and blessings of Allah be upon you all.

First of all, I would like to take this opportunity to express my heartfelt gratitude and thanks to all of our guests who have taken the time to join us here today. Your attendance is noteworthy and commendable given that you are attending a religious community's function, at a time when interest in religion is on the decline in much of the world.

It is of even greater note that you are attending a Muslim event, where a new mosque is being inaugurated, despite the fact that most of you are non-Muslims and have no religious or emotional affiliation with mosques or with Islam. Indeed, we are all well aware that, regrettably, we live in a time where many people hold reservations, and even fears, about Islam and about Muslims. In light of all of this, undoubtedly your attendance is praiseworthy and obliges me to profess my deepest gratitude to all of you.

Moreover, I should clarify that my thanks is not offered as a mere courtesy, rather it is a religious duty placed on me by Islam, as the Prophet of Islam, the Holy Prophet Muhammad[sas], taught that a person who fails to express his appreciation to other people cannot be grateful to God Almighty. Hence, I consider it my religious obligation to express my sincere gratitude to all of you.

Moving on, I anticipate that you will have joined us today in the hope of learning more about Islam and to find out the reasons why we have built this mosque. Certainly, given the fact that many people have misgivings about Islam due to what they have seen in the media, such curiosity and interest is natural. Indeed, due to the climate in which we are living, if you harbour any fears or concerns about this mosque, it is quite understandable.

Undoubtedly, in much of the world, there is now an increasingly prevalent view that Muslims are to be feared. As a collective, Muslims have been branded as troublemakers who seek to divide society and desire to shatter the fabric of social cohesion and peace. Muslims are seen as people who are neither able to live together in peace nor are they able to live peacefully with others. Further, the construction of a mosque is something that evokes even greater fear and anxiety amongst many non-Muslims. Many people fear that a mosque will provide Muslims with a centre to isolate themselves from the rest of society and to undermine the peace and well-being of the local town, city or even of the nation itself. I have personally seen that such fears do exist amongst many people in the non-Muslim world and, regrettably, such angst and suspicion of Islam and its followers continues to rise.

Nevertheless, the truth is, and will always remain, that Islam is completely opposed to all forms of extremism, terrorism or violence. It condemns, in the strongest possible terms, any attempts to violate freedom of belief and freedom of conscience. Under no circumstances does Islam permit coercion or force in the matter of religion; rather, Islam teaches that religion is a matter of the heart, as is written in the Holy Quran. Thus, I firmly believe that the widespread and common perceptions of Islam amongst non-Muslims are actually misconceptions. In terms of any mosque, it is vital to look at its true objectives, according to the teachings of Islam.

What do Muslims—true Muslims I should say—intend when they build mosques? If a person judiciously assesses the objectives of a mosque and the reasons why they are considered to be sacred places to Muslims, they will soon realise that true mosques are not there to be feared. In order to alleviate any apprehensions that may exist amongst the local community, I shall now briefly mention the core purposes, so that you can all better understand what this new mosque and indeed all true mosques represent.

A primary objective of a mosque is, of course, the worship of the One God and so mosques are a place where Muslims join together to bow down and prostrate before God Almighty in worship. Such worship is offered five times a day and is known as *Salat*. This is a fundamental pillar of faith for every Muslim, which he or she must observe. A second crucial purpose of a mosque is to be a place for Muslims who join together for worship, to be able to strengthen their mutual relations and to develop unity amongst the community members. Hence, through their mosques, Muslims are able to forge greater ties of kinship and to establish an atmosphere of brotherhood and mutual sympathy.

The third pivotal objective for any mosque is to be a means of introducing non-Muslims to the teachings of Islam and to fulfil the rights of the wider society. It is to provide a platform and venue from which Muslims can join together to serve their local community and to help all members of society, regardless of creed, caste or colour. Chapter 4, verse 37 of the Holy Quran, states:

> And worship Allah and associate naught with Him, and *show* kindness to parents, and to kindred, and orphans, and the needy, and to the neighbour who is a kinsman and the neighbour who is a stranger, and the companion by *your* side, and the wayfarer, and those whom your right hands possess. Surely, Allah loves not the arrogant *and* the boastful.

In this verse, the Holy Quran instructs Muslims to show kindness and compassion to a whole range of people. It calls on them to serve their parents, family members, other relatives and also vulnerable members of society. It also places great emphasis on fulfilling the rights of one's neighbours. Neighbours are not just people who live in a person's immediate vicinity; rather, the scope of neighbours in Islam is extremely far-reaching and includes those who live near, as well as those who live at a distance. It includes a person's colleagues, his travel companions, and much more besides these. Therefore, in essence, all of the people of this city are the neighbours of this mosque. Thus, instead of destroying the peace of society, true mosques are built to foster peace between the peoples of different communities and beliefs.

In short, mosques are a place for Muslims to elevate their bond with their Creator, God Almighty, and to fulfil the rights of their fellow human beings. Any mosques that do not fulfil these paramount objectives are worthless and merely hollow shells that serve no purpose. Since its foundation, the Ahmadiyya Muslim Community has built mosques across the world and our history testifies to the fact that, wherever we build mosques, we endeavour to fulfil the objectives that I have just outlined. Through our conduct and behaviour, we seek to practically manifest and live up to our community's slogan of, 'Love for All, Hatred for None'.

We seek to build ties of friendship with non-Ahmadis and non-Muslims. We strive for interfaith dialogue.

We value and cherish our neighbours.

We are ever ready to help those who are in need.

We champion the rights of the weak and deprived.

We are there to serve the community and to be loyal and faithful citizens.

This is our faith and this is our teaching.

This is why we build mosques.

In light of this, I hope and pray that it is clear to all of you that a mosque is not something to be afraid of. A true mosque is not just a centre for people to worship God Almighty, but is also a stage for them to serve their fellow beings. Chapter 107, verses 5–7 of the Holy Quran state:

So woe to those who pray, but are unmindful of their
Prayer. They only like to be seen *of men*.

These verses categorically declare that the prayers of those people who worship God, but who fail to discharge the rights owed
to His Creation, will be rejected. Their worship and entry into a
mosque is nothing but an act and a superficial gesture. The Holy
Quran is very clear that their prayers are meaningless and their
hypocritical ways will lead only to their disgrace and despair.
Consequently, the reality is that true Muslims, who worship Allah
the Almighty with sincerity, can never do anything that harms, or
negatively affects, the peace and well-being of a society. Nor can
they seek to undermine or seize the rights of other people, because
to do so would be to betray their faith and to abandon the teachings of the Holy Quran and of the Holy Prophet Muhammad[sas].

Thus, let me once again reassure you about this mosque. You
have no reason to be anxious or concerned. The doors to this
mosque will be forever open to all peace-loving people.

They will always be open to those who value humanity. I am
entirely confident that, God Willing, this mosque will prove to
be a symbol of peace, radiating nothing but love, compassion and
brotherhood throughout the city and far beyond.

It will serve as a beacon illuminating its surroundings and
spreading light in every direction. It will be a House of Peace in
which the worshippers join together to serve their neighbours
and to fulfil their rights. It will represent the enlightened teachings of Islam and dispel all fears and myths that exist about our
religion. God Willing, any lingering fears that may remain in the
hearts and minds of the local community will vanish altogether.

When they see this mosque or meet the people who worship here, they will soon realise that there is no need for any apprehension or trepidation.

Whilst it is easy to make such statements, I am convinced you will soon attest yourselves to the fact that Ahmadi Muslim practice what they preach and are people who not only proclaim Islam's teachings of peace, but who uphold them. It is my firm belief that the local community will soon realise that what I have said about the objectives of mosques are not sugar-coated words masking a bitter pill, but represent the honest truth.

At this time, I would also like to say that it is up to all members of society, whether Muslim or non-Muslim, whether religious or non-religious, to work together for the peace and prosperity of the world. Rather than making allegations against one another, or pinpointing each other's flaws and weaknesses, we should open our hearts to others and show grace and compassion. Instead of attacking each other's religions and needlessly provoking one another, it is the urgent need of the time that we exhibit mutual respect and tolerance. True and long-lasting peace cannot suddenly develop with the click of our fingers; rather, it requires us to focus upon those things that unite us and which bring us together, rather than letting our differences divide us and break our societies.

I truly believe that we are passing through a critical juncture in the history of the world where, both at a national and international level, the world is becoming increasingly polarised and divided.

We stand upon the brink of disaster and so now is the time to take a step back and focus all of our energies on protecting the future of mankind. Now is the time to show our humanity and to spare no efforts in developing peace in our communities, in our nations and indeed throughout the world. Only if we come together and respect each other's beliefs, can we begin to heal the bitter rifts that have taken root in much of the world. Only then can we bequeath a legacy of hope for our children. Only then will we leave behind a prosperous and peaceful world for the coming generations.

We must not be blinded by self-interest and greed, rather we must open our eyes and look to the common good. It is my sincere hope and prayer that all of us, no matter our religion or beliefs, can work together with a spirit of benevolence and mutual respect and that our shared ambition is to make the world a better place for those who follow us. Our common goal should be to foster peace, harmony and goodwill between the people of all communities and we should constantly aspire to and strive to leave behind a peaceful world for our children in which people are able to live side by side, irrespective of differences of race, religion or belief.

May Allah the Almighty enable us to all work together for the betterment of mankind—*Aameen.*

At the end, I would like to thank you all once again for joining us.

May Allah the Almighty bless all of you.

Thank you very much.

SERVING HUMANITY—
A FORM OF WORSHIP OF ALLAH

INAUGURATION OF THE NASIR HOSPITAL

HUMANITY FIRST, GUATEMALA

OCTOBER 23, 2018

Hazrat Mirza Masroor Ahmad, Khalifatul-Masih V^aba, Addresses the Guest Reception at Nasir Hospital's Inauguration

Hazrat Mirza Masroor Ahmad, Khalifatul-Masih V^aba, Leads Guests of the Nasir Hospital Inauguration in Silent Prayers. Special guests seated include: Miguel Figueroa, Vice Minister of Health, Guatemala; Naftaly Aldana, Magistrate Judge, Constitutional Court of Guatemala; Iliana Dominguez, Member of Guatemala Congress; Sergio Celis, Member of Guatemala Congress; Honourable Norma Torres, Member United States Congress; and Honourable David Hodge, Charge d'affaires, U.S. Embassy Guatemala

Hazrat Mirza Masroor Ahmad, Khalifatul-Masih V^aba Meets with U.S. Congresswoman Norma Torres

Hazrat Mirza Masroor Ahmad, Khalifatul-Masih V^aba Cuts Ribbon Inaugurating Nasir Hospital

Preface

On 23rd October 2018, the Head of the Worldwide Ahmadiyya Muslim Community, the Fifth Khalifah, His Holiness Hazrat Mirza Masroor Ahmad[aba], delivered the keynote address at a special reception held to mark the historic inauguration of the Nasir Hospital, a large-scale humanitarian project of Humanity First, an international charity established by the Ahmadiyya Muslim Community. Eight hundred dignitaries and guests, representing twenty countries, attended the reception held at the hospital, located in Sacatepéquez, Guatemala. His Holiness met with a range of dignitaries, including Congresswoman Norma Torres from the United States, Miguel Figueroa, Vice Minister of Health, Guatemala, and Iliana Dominguez, Member of Congress, Guatemala. A range of dignitaries also addressed the audience. They included US Congresswoman Norma Torres and Vice Minister of Health Guatemala, Miguel Figueroa. His Holiness also answered questions during a press conference with the assembled media.

SERVING HUMANITY—
A FORM OF WORSHIP OF ALLAH

After reciting tashahhud, ta'awwuz and bismillaah, Hazrat Mirza Masroor Ahmad^aba, the Head of the Worldwide Ahmadiyya Muslim Community, said:

—◦⊱✦⊰◦—

All distinguished guests, *Assalaamo alaikum wa Rahmatullaahe wa Barakaatohu*—peace and blessings of Allah be upon you all.

Firstly, I would like to express my sincere gratitude to all of our guests who are attending today's event here in Guatemala. Undoubtedly, today is a source of great joy and delight for members of the Ahmadiyya Muslim Community, as the very first hospital built by Humanity First, in either Central or South America, is being inaugurated. In this regard, we consider it to be an extremely significant and landmark occasion.

Whilst Humanity First is an independent charity and has its own mandate and strategies, at the same time, it was originally founded by the Ahmadiyya Muslim Community and continues to be managed by Ahmadi Muslims. Through financial contributions and other means, Ahmadi Muslims across the globe support the efforts of Humanity First, so that it can increase the scope of its humanitarian projects and further its reach. Thus, Humanity First has a deep and lasting connection with the Ahmadiyya Muslim Community, and so today is not only a day of happiness for the members of Humanity First, but for Ahmadi Muslims worldwide.

You may well be wondering why we have built this hospital. The answer is very simple. It has been built with purely one intention, and that is, quite simply, to serve humanity by providing high quality healthcare to the people of this nation. Also, I wish to clarify at the outset that having built this institute, this will not be the end of our services to this country; rather, it is my prayer that this proves to be the first of many humanitarian projects established by Humanity First in this region. Indeed, I hope and pray that the opening of the hospital serves as a launch pad, propelling Humanity First towards furthering their mission of providing relief, support, and opportunities to people throughout the world.

Perhaps some of our guests may be surprised, or even perplexed, as to why a Muslim community has so much passion and determination to help and serve non-Muslims. To answer this question, I should explain that ever since its foundation, the Ahmadiyya Muslim Community has always sought to be on the very front lines of serving humanity, whether it be directly through our own Community's schemes, or through Humanity First or through the support of other charities and good causes. For example, over the past few decades, the Ahmadiyya Muslim Community has opened many hospitals and schools across Africa, in which the local people are provided access to healthcare and excellent education, irrespective of their ethnicity, religion or social background. Most of the patients treated at our hospitals in Africa are non-Muslims and around 90% of the students who study in our schools are non-Muslims. Thus, we do not discriminate against any community or people and do not give any priority to our own members.

In terms of education, the schooling we provide is from primary age all the way up to higher secondary education. Our objective is for all children to be literate and to have a firm educational foundation, upon which they can build their future lives. Furthermore, we also provide scholarships for talented students, who otherwise would not have the means for higher studies, so they can fulfil their potential and build a better future for themselves, for their people and for their nation. Accordingly, the Ahmadiyya Muslim Community, whether directly, or whether through Humanity First or otherwise, has a long history of serving humanity, of providing opportunities and offering comfort and help to people who are living impoverished lives.

We seek no praise and no reward for such efforts because we are merely doing what our religion has taught us to do. Our motivation and our desire to serve others is driven entirely by the teachings of Islam. The guiding light for any true Muslim is the Holy Quran, which was revealed to Islam's Founder, the Holy Prophet Muhammad[sas]. Time and again, the Holy Quran has instructed Muslims to serve mankind and to fulfil the needs of those who are suffering, or are deprived in any way. It requires Muslims to be selfless and consumed by a love for others. It requires us to be everready to make sacrifices for the sake of the peace and well-being of other people.

For example, in chapter 3, verse 111, Allah the Almighty has stated that a Muslim is he who 'enjoins what is good and forbids evil.' Here, the Quran explains that true Muslims are people who promote goodness, stay away from evil and injustice and encourage others to do good deeds as well. Only a person who has a sincere love for humankind and feels the anguish of God's creation can be caring and sympathetic, in the way the Quran desires. Such profound love for humanity is only possible if your heart is pure and free from malice and selfishness.

In chapter 2, verse 84 of the Holy Quran, Allah the Almighty instructs Muslims to speak kindly at all times, to be considerate of the feelings of other people and to love and protect vulnerable members of society, such as orphan children or those living in poverty or destitution. Thereafter, in chapter 51, verse 20, the Holy Quran states that the hallmark of a true Muslim is that he should care for all of God's creation and should comfort and support those in need, whether they seek their help or not. Hence, it is not enough for a Muslim to wait until someone asks for help; rather, it is his duty to recognise the suffering of others and to make whatever sacrifices are required in order to help them overcome their challenges or troubles.

Further, in chapter 90, verses 15–17, Muslims are instructed to feed the hungry, to show empathy and love to orphans, and to help anyone in need, especially those mired in poverty or who are defenceless and weak. Muslims are taught to be the ones who comfort and love those people who have been failed by society and to carry the weight of their burdens on their own shoulders. Muslims are duty-bound to help underprivileged people, so that they can stand upon their own two feet, live with dignity, and be freed from their desperate circumstances. In return, the Quran states Muslims will be rewarded with increased spirituality, which in turn will take them towards God Almighty and make them recipients of His pleasure.

Similarly, in chapter 2, verse 196, the Holy Quran states that if a person wishes to save himself from humiliation, degradation and ruin, he must be kind, generous and do good to others, without expectation of anything in return. Chapter 4, verse 37 of the Holy Quran states that Muslims should care for their neighbours and reiterates that it is the duty of a true Muslim to fulfil the rights of the needy and orphans. It instructs Muslims to be benevolent and to treat anyone under their supervision with love, patience, and affection. For example, if a Muslim has a subordinate at work, they should treat them with kindness and generosity. Furthermore, in chapter 47, verse 39 of the Holy Quran, Allah the Almighty instructs Muslims to spend their wealth for the sake of helping others. Those who are unwilling to do so have been declared as niggardly and the Quran states that such miserly ways are not liked by Allah and are a means of darkening a person's soul.

All the verses I have quoted emphasise the fact that, if Muslims desire to attain the love of Allah the Almighty, they must first show love to the creation of God. The verses clearly illustrate that the very foundation and bedrock of Islam is service to humanity. My purpose in sharing these Quranic quotes is so that you all know that Islam is not what is commonly portrayed in the media. It is not a religion of extremism, violence, or terrorism; rather, it is a religion of love, compassion, and tolerance. It is a religion that considers service to humanity as a fundamental obligation placed upon its followers. Thus, how could it be possible that a true Muslim be hard-hearted or fail to help those who are suffering or facing any type of hardship?

Having given some Quranic references, let me present the example of the Founder of Islam, the Holy Prophet Muhammad[sas], with regard to service to humanity. In the modern era, it is often alleged that the Holy Prophet Muhammad[sas] was a belligerent leader who encouraged his followers to be violent. However, let it be crystal clear that this is a grave injustice made against his blessed character and nothing could be further from the truth. The Prophet of Islam[sas] championed the rights of all people, of all races and of all beliefs and was a source of unparalleled mercy and grace for all mankind. From every pore and fibre of his being gushed forth an eternal spring of love and compassion for humanity. For example, on one occasion, the Holy Prophet Muhammad[sas] said: 'I am with the weak because aiding the weak and poor is the means of reaching Allah the Almighty.'

Furthermore, the Prophet of Islam[sas] taught that Allah the Almighty was most pleased by those who helped the poor, who filled their empty stomachs and who arranged medical treatment for them. Hence, if a person claims to be a true Muslim, it is his obligation and overriding duty to assist all those who are facing difficulties and to strive to alleviate their distress and heartache. In the modern era, the person who according to our faith was sent by Allah the Almighty to enlighten the world of the true teachings of Islam, was the Founder of the Ahmadiyya Muslim Community, whom we believe to be the Promised Messiah and Imam Mahdi [Guided One]. He was sent to show the world what Islam truly is and to propagate its teachings to all parts of the world.

Where he came to enlighten non-Muslims about Islam, he also came to reform the Muslims themselves, who had forgotten the original teachings of their faith and bring them back towards the Islam taught by the Holy Quran and the Holy Prophet Muhammad[sas]. Above all, he constantly drew the attention of mankind towards fulfilling both the rights of God Almighty and of one another. On one occasion, the Promised Messiah[as] said: Serving humanity is itself a form of worship [of Allah].

At another place, the Promised Messiah[as] said: My state is such that if someone is in distress, whilst I am engaged in the obligatory prayers and I hear their grief, it is my ardent desire to break the prayer and to try to help that person and to shower them with as much love as possible.

The Promised Messiah[as] further said: To fail to help a brother in their time of need or difficulty is utterly immoral and wrong.

Furthermore, the Promised Messiah[as] said that, if a person did not have the material means to help someone struggling or facing difficulties, they should, at the very least, fervently pray that Allah the Almighty remove their problems. He taught that sincere prayer required a soft and pure heart and so Muslims had a duty to be sympathetic to the plight of others and to consider their trials as though they were their own.

On another occasion, the Promised Messiah[as] said: More than anyone else, I implore people to manifest the highest morals and love towards non-Muslims, such as Hindus.

The Promised Messiah[as] said: Treat all the creation of God with such deep love as though they are your close family members. Treat mankind in the same way that a mother treats her child. This is the way you should be and not that you help someone only so that you can attain benefit later or take a favour in return.

Similarly, the Promised Messiah[as] has said: In chapter 16, verse 91 of the Holy Quran, Allah the Almighty has instructed Muslims to act with justice and to do good to all others. Hence, you must treat even those people with love who have done no good to you. In fact, you should go beyond this and favour them and care for them as a mother cares for her child.

What a magnificent and noble teaching! We have all seen and felt the pure love that a mother has for her child. A mother has no expectation of reward, nor does she seek any recognition. All the while, she loves her child more than she loves herself and never weakens in her resolve to nourish and protect her offspring. It is this mother-like spirit of selflessness that Islam requires Muslims to develop in their hearts for all of humanity and not just their own progeny. In practical terms, the Promised Messiah[as] wasted no opportunity to serve others.

For example, he lived in a very small village in India in the 19th Century, where there were no proper medical facilities available. Thus, out of a desire to serve humanity, the Promised Messiah[as] studied traditional native medicine and would keep a stock of such medication in his home. As a result, the local people would visit him and, irrespective of their caste, creed or colour, he would distribute medicines to them according to their needs. Many people, especially the poorest and most deprived members of society, benefitted greatly from this provision. The only desire and objective of the Promised Messiah[as] was to serve humanity, and this was the great treasure and legacy that he left behind for his community.

Thus, the efforts of the Ahmadiyya Muslim Community to serve humanity in all parts of the world are entirely motivated out of a desire to ease the sufferings of mankind and this is why Humanity First is today opening its first hospital in this part of the world. With all my heart, I hope and pray that it fulfils its mandate and proves an exceptional means of alleviating the suffering of people, regardless of their religious beliefs, regardless of their age and regardless of their ethnic or social backgrounds. As I have said, we desire no reward or praise from the world, our only target is to seek the love and favour of God Almighty.

We are forever inspired by the words of the Promised Messiah[as], who said that serving humanity was the means of fulfilling the true purpose of our lives and attaining the blessings and bounties of God Almighty. I am confident it will now be clear to all of you that we have not constructed this hospital in order to profit, or to gain favourable publicity; rather, our only objective is to serve the people of your nation, by providing high-quality healthcare to the people of this land.

Rest assured, any funds generated by the hospital will be used to further serve the people of Guatemala and not a penny will be sent abroad. Whatever income is received through patient fees will be reinvested to ensure that those who cannot afford treatment can receive it at a subsidised rate or, if feasible, for free. Apart from this, any additional income will be used to maintain and improve the hospital facilities or to fund new ways to serve humanity. Our previous humanitarian projects testify to the truth of what I have said.

Wherever we have built schools or hospitals, we have never taken any of the income out of the country; rather, we have always reinvested it locally in a way that benefits the people of that nation—and the same will be the case here in Guatemala. God willing, this is not the end of our commitment to serving this nation, but is only the start. Certainly, it is my prayer and sincere hope that this hospital is the first of many humanitarian projects that we establish in this part of the world. I pray that we always continue to increase our efforts to fulfil our duty and responsibility to serve humanity.

It is my prayer that Allah the Almighty blesses the hospital in all respects, enables it to go from strength to strength and that it proves a shining example of service to humanity. I pray that it provides the best possible care for patients and that the doctors and staff work tirelessly for the sake of providing relief to people, especially to those who are poor and deprived.

May Allah the Almighty bless the work of the doctors and medical staff and enable them to heal and cure through His grace. It is my prayer that the administration manages the hospital in a way that the poorest people, who cannot otherwise afford treatment, are offered heavily subsidised care and, wherever possible, free treatment.

This hospital has been named the 'Nasir Hospital', and 'Nasir' means to help and support others, and so I pray that the hospital forever lives up to its name in all respects. I pray that it develops into an outstanding institution, known for its high calibre and, above all, for its unrelenting commitment to helping the most vulnerable members of society.

At the end, I pray that all people, irrespective of religion, race or ethnicity, join together in the service of humanity and work towards the betterment of society, with a spirit of love and cooperation.

Today's world has become like a global village, as every nation is now inter-connected and the means of communication are instantaneous. As a result, more than ever before, it is the duty of all humankind to foster a spirit of brotherhood and mutual love amongst the peoples of all nations and of all beliefs.

Regrettably, the sad truth remains that instead of elevating our standards of love and compassion, the opposite is proving true. Selfishness, greed and a culture of 'me', is prevailing across the world and across society. Thus, I pray with all my heart, that mankind forsakes greed and forgoes the pursuit of narrow self-interests, and instead comes to recognise the importance of protecting all of humanity and of showing kindness, compassion and love to God's creation.

I pray that a spirit of service to humanity takes permanent root in society, so that we protect our future and leave behind a better world for our children and coming generations to live in. May Allah the Almighty enable all of us to fulfil our responsibilities in this regard, *Aameen*.

With these words, I would like to once again thank all of our guests for joining us at today's event.

Thank you very much.

RELIGIOUS TOLERANCE AND FREEDOM IN ISLAM

INAUGURATION OF THE MASROOR MOSQUE
MANASSAS, VIRGINIA, USA
NOVEMBER 3, 2018

Hazrat Mirza Masroor Ahmad, Khalifatul-Masih V^aba Receives a Special Bi-Partisan Resolution
from U.S. Congress for His U.S. Tour Presented by U.S. Congressman Gerry Connolly

Hazrat Mirza Masroor Ahmad, Khalifatul-Masih V^{aba} Receives a Special Recognition from the Governor of Virginia, Ralph Northam, Presented by Honourable Hala Ayala (Member, Virginia House of Delegates) and Honourable Jeremy McPike (Member, Virginia State Senate)

Hazrat Mirza Masroor Ahmad, Khalifatul-Masih V^{aba} Leads Guests of the Masroor Mosque Reception in Silent Prayers. Special Guests Seated Include Honourable Hala Ayala (Member, Virginia House of Delegates), Honourable Dawda Fadera (Gambia Ambassador to the United States), Dr Katrina Lantos Swett (President, Lantos Foundation for Human Rights and Justice), Honourable Gerry Connolly (U.S. Congressman) and Jeremy McPike (Member, Virginia State Senate)

Preface

On Saturday 3rd November, 2018, the Head of the Worldwide Ahmadiyya Muslim Community, the Fifth Khalifah, His Holiness Hazrat Mirza Masroor Ahmad[aba], inaugurated the Masroor Mosque in Manassas, Virginia, USA. A reception was held in the evening in which over 200 dignitaries and guests attended. Hala Ayala, member of the Virginia House of Delegates who was representing the 51st district of Virginia, which includes Masroor Mosque, presented His Holiness with a certificate of recognition on behalf of the Governor of Virginia, Ralph Northam. Some of the dignitaries delivered brief remarks to the audience including Gerry Connolly, member of the United States Congress for Virginia's 11th District and Dr Katrina Lantos Swett, President of the Lantos Foundation for Human Rights and Justice and former Chair of the United States Commission on International Religious Freedom.

RELIGIOUS TOLERANCE AND
FREEDOM IN ISLAM

After reciting tashahhud, ta'awwuz and bismillaah, Hazrat Mirza Masroor Ahmad[aba], the Head of the Worldwide Ahmadiyya Muslim Community, said:

—◦⫸◈⫷◦—

All distinguished guests, *Assalaamo alaikum wa Rahmatullaahe wa Barakaatohu*—peace and blessings of Allah be upon you all.

Before proceeding further, I would like to take this opportunity to sincerely thank all of our guests, for having accepted our invitation and joining us at the opening of this mosque.

It is actually my religious duty to express my sincere gratitude to you, because the Founder of Islam, the Holy Prophet Muhammad[sas], taught that a person who was not grateful to his fellow human beings could not be grateful to God Almighty. The vast majority of people living in this city are non-Muslims and the number of Ahmadi Muslims in this area is very small.

However, irrespective of our small numbers, the county officials and local people have permitted us to build this mosque and this demonstrates your open hearts and high levels of tolerance. In addition, the fact that you are joining us at this Islamic religious event, even though most of you are not Muslims, reflects your open-mindedness and it is because of your tolerant nature that you are able to successfully absorb and integrate new communities into the local society.

In this era, we are all aware that Muslims and Islam generally receive a great deal of negative media attention. A major cause of the adverse coverage is that a small minority of so-called Muslims have been radicalised and behaved in a truly reprehensible way, whilst trying to justify their hate-filled acts in the name of Islam. As a result, many non-Muslims have reservations and fears about Islam.

In fact, increasingly, people consider it as a threat to society and a religion that promotes extremism and violence. In light of this, the fact that the local community approved the building of this mosque, and the fact that you are all joining us in our celebration, is extremely praiseworthy and obliges me to once again express my sincere appreciation and heartfelt gratitude to you all. I also wish to reassure you that the negative media portrayal of Islam is completely at odds with the reality of the religion.

The despicable acts of certain groups or individuals who use Islam's name to justify violence and extremism have nothing to do with the true teachings of Islam. Islam's teachings are of peace, love, reconciliation and brotherhood. In fact, the literal meaning of the Arabic word 'Islam' is 'peace'. When the very name and foundation of a religion is peace, it is impossible for that religion to promote or permit anything that undermines the peace and well-being of society.

Rather, the teachings of such a religion must foster peace and spread love and compassion amongst humanity. Certainly, this is what we have learned from the Holy Quran, which is our Holy Book and the most authentic source of Islamic law and teaching. From cover to cover, the Holy Quran is a book of peace that enshrines universal human values and human rights. Its teachings seek to unite mankind under the banner of humanity and guarantee the rights of every individual to live with freedom, equality, liberty and justice.

It is written in the Holy Quran that Allah the Almighty sent Prophets to the world in order for them to instil basic human values and to teach morality. They were sent to develop a relationship between God Almighty and His creation and to draw the attention of mankind towards fulfilling the rights of one another. As Muslims, we believe that in order to fulfil these great objectives, God Almighty sent His Messengers to all nations and the history of the major religions testifies to the fact that all the Prophets practised and preached the highest standards of morality and virtue.

Hence, Islam's teachings unite mankind and foster a spirit of mutual love and respect between all people, irrespective of racial, religious or social backgrounds. It is a religion that breaks down barriers and encourages peaceful and tolerant dialogue. Thus, it is inconceivable for a true Muslim to persecute or oppose other religions or their followers. At no place, and at no time, has Islam ever promoted extremism or encouraged violence in any shape or form.

Wherever and whenever a Muslim has conducted a terrorist attack or exhibited any type of radicalism or fanatical behaviour, it is only because he or she has deviated entirely from Islam's teachings. Such people, and such acts, serve only to defame and besmirch the pure name of Islam. In the very first chapter of the Holy Quran, Allah the Almighty has proclaimed that He is the 'Lord of All the Worlds', Who provides for and sustains all mankind.

This means that God is the Provider and Sustainer of all people, irrespective of their faith or beliefs. Due to the grace and benevolence of God Almighty, even those who deny His existence or have no religion are reaping the blessings and fruits of this world. Accordingly, where the Quran declares Allah the Almighty to be the 'Lord of all the worlds' it also proclaims Him to be the Gracious and the Merciful. Similarly, in the Holy Quran, Allah the Almighty has proclaimed the Founder of Islam, the Holy Prophet Muhammad[sas], as 'a mercy for all mankind'.

Without a shadow of a doubt, at every moment of his life, the Prophet of Islam[sas] manifested immense love and respect for all people. His pure and noble heart was filled with compassion and, at all times, he sought the betterment of mankind and strived to alleviate the suffering of others. He taught his followers to respect and value all humanity. For example, on one occasion, the Holy Prophet Muhammad[sas] was sitting down, but immediately stood up as a mark of respect when he observed a funeral procession pass by. Upon this, one of his companions mentioned that the deceased was a Jewish person and not a Muslim. Hearing this, the Prophet of Islam[sas] asked, 'Was he not a human?'

This reflected the love in his heart for all humanity. It also manifests how he guided his followers towards treating the people of all religions and beliefs with compassion and being sensitive and respectful to their feelings and needs. Furthermore, many people question whether Islam advocates freedom of religion. To

answer this, let me present another incident from the time of the
Holy Prophet Muhammad[sas].

Once, a delegation of Christians from the Arab city of Najran
came to meet the Holy Prophet Muhammad[sas] in Madinah.
After some time, the Christians became restless and so the Holy
Prophet[sas] enquired if something was wrong. In response, the
Christians informed him that it was time for their worship, but
they did not have an appropriate place to perform their prayers or
rituals. Upon this, the Prophet of Islam[sas] invited the Christians
to worship in his own mosque in Madinah, according to their traditions and ways.

Through this munificent and magnanimous gesture, the
Holy Prophet Muhammad[sas] set an everlasting example of tolerance, freedom of religion and freedom of worship for all mankind. Nevertheless, some people question why wars or battles
were fought by the early Muslims. Thus, let me make it clear that
wherever Islam permitted the use of force, it was never to conquer
lands or to compel people to accept Islam; rather, where the Holy
Quran authorised the early Muslims to utilise a degree of force, it
clearly stipulated that permission was granted in order to establish
peace and security and to ensure that true freedom of religion and
freedom of belief prevailed.

It explained that the use of force was not given to save Islam,
but was given in order to protect the rights of all people and religions and to guarantee the rights of all communities to believe
as they pleased. Consequently, in chapter 22, verse 41 of the
Holy Quran, where permission was first granted to the Muslims
to engage in a defensive war, it clarified that the opponents of
Islam were not waging war against the Muslims for any personal,

national or political reasons; rather, they were motivated by their hatred of religion itself.

The verse warned that if the Muslims did not take firm steps to stop the cruelties and injustice, it would lead to the end of all religions and freedom of belief would cease to exist. The verse categorically says that churches, synagogues, temples, mosques or any other places of worship, would not be safe if they were permitted to wage war if their attacks were not retaliated.

Thus, rather than imposing restrictions or curtailing freedoms, the truth is that the world's first and foremost universal charter of religious freedom was the Holy Quran itself. Moreover, as Islam has enshrined freedom of belief as a basic human right, it naturally follows that true mosques are symbols of religious freedom and shining beacons of love, mutual respect and compassion.

Certainly, I hope and expect that in your interactions with Ahmadi Muslims in the past, you will only have felt a spirit of love and respect from them towards you. Now this mosque has been officially opened, this spirit will only increase and our message of peace and humanity will reverberate ever louder and echo in all directions. The local Ahmadi Muslims will intensify their efforts to fulfil the rights of the neighbours of this mosque.

Indeed, the Holy Quran has repeatedly instructed Muslims to fulfil the rights of their neighbours and to treat them with the utmost love and affection. I should clarify that our neighbours are not only those who live close to the mosque or close to the homes of Ahmadi Muslims; rather, the circle of neighbours, according to the Holy Quran, spreads much further afield and includes a person's colleagues, subordinates, travel companions and many other people besides. In essence, all the people of this city are our neighbours and it is our religious obligation to treat them with love, kindness and generosity.

I pray the local Ahmadi Muslims live up to what I have said and personally reflect Islam's core message of love and humanity through their words and conduct, each and every day. May they convey Islam's message of peace and goodwill, not only in the local area, but across the nation as well.

May the local Ahmadi Muslims treat their neighbours and all other members of society with love and empathy, so that whatever fears or reservations exist about Islam in the minds of some non-Muslims, soon disappear. I pray the noble teachings of our most sacred book, the Holy Quran, are exhibited by our Ahmadi Muslims so that the local people can see what Islam truly is.

May the benevolent and peaceful character of the Holy Prophet Muhammad[sas], who was the perfect manifestation of the Quran's teachings, be revealed to the people here in the United States and beyond. It is also my heartfelt prayer that all people of all beliefs, whether at a local, regional, national or international level, unite in a common purpose of spreading peace in the world.

From the depths of my heart, I pray that after we have departed this world, our children and future generations remember us with love and affection. May they affirm that their elders spared no effort to foster a spirit of love, peace and brotherhood amongst mankind and to leave behind a peaceful and enlightened world. Surely, the alternative does not bear thinking about – that our children remember us with nothing but contempt and consider us to have been belligerent warmongers, who destroyed their futures and left behind only a trail of war and destruction.

Thus, in order to protect our future generations, it is essential we set aside our differences and focus on fulfilling each other's rights and serving humanity. It is our responsibility, and indeed our obligation, to ensure we leave behind a peaceful and prosperous world for those that follow us. To achieve this great objective we must be ready to expend all our energies on striving for peace. A fundamental principle of Islam is to hold all religions and their founders in great esteem. As I said at the beginning, we believe in all of the prophets, and so it is not possible for a true Muslim to ever speak against them or their teachings.

Hence, it is of paramount importance that, irrespective of a person's race or social status, we respect one another's beliefs and religions. With these words, I hope and pray that may Allah the Almighty enable us all to play our respective roles in bringing an end to the conflicts that have plagued the world and to eradicate all forms of injustice and intolerance. Rather than a world of hate and hostility, I pray we leave behind a world of love and compassion.

Instead of selfishly pursuing self-interests, may all people recognise the true value of serving the common good. At the end, I pray that this mosque proves to be a shining light in this community and a means of unity and hope—*Aameen*.

Thank you all once again for joining us today.

May God bless you all.

Thank you.

U.S. CONGRESS— HOUSE RESOLUTION 1125

To honour the historic U.S. visit of Hazrat Mirza Masroor Ahmad, Khalifatul-Masih V^(aba), nineteen members of the U.S. Congress co-sponsored a bi-partisan resolution before the U.S. House of Representatives.

MEMBERS OF THE U.S. CONGRESS SUPPORTING
THE RESOLUTION

	MEMBER NAME	AFFILIATION-STATE
1	U.S. Congressman Peter King	Republican—New York *Ahmadiyya Muslim Caucus Co-Chair
2	U.S. Congresswoman Jackie Speier	Democrat—California *Ahmadiyya Muslim Caucus Co-Chair
3	U.S. Congressman Frank Pallone	Democrat—New Jersey
4	U.S. Congressman James McGovern	Democrat—Massachusetts
5	U.S. Congressman Peter Roskam	Republican—Illinois
6	U.S. Congressman Ted Poe	Republican—Texas
7	U.S. Congressman Pete Aguilar	Democrat—California

MEMBER NAME	AFFILIATION-STATE
8 U.S. CONGRESSMAN Jamie Raskin	Democrat—Maryland
9 U.S. Congresswoman Norma Torres	Democrat—California
10 U.S. Congressman Michael McCaul	Republican—Texas
11 U.S. Congressman Gerry Connolly	Democrat—Virginia
12 U.S. Congresswoman Zoe Lofgren	Democrat—California
13 U.S. Congressman Brad Sherman	Democrat—California
14 U.S. Congresswoman Gwen Moore	Democrat—California
15 U.S. Congresswoman Judy Chu	Democrat—California
16 U.S. Congressman Tom Suozzi	Democrat—New York
17 U.S. Congressman Raja Krishnamoorthi	Democrat—Illinois
18 U.S. Congressman Andre Carson	Democrat—Indiana
19 U.S. Congresswoman Suzanne Bonamici	Democrat—Oregon

115TH CONGRESS
2D SESSION

H. RES. 1125

Welcoming His Holiness, Hadhrat Mirza Masroor Ahmad, the worldwide spiritual head of the Ahmadiyya Muslim Community, to the United States, including Pennsylvania, Maryland, Texas, Virginia, and Washington, DC, and recognizing his commitment to world peace, absolute justice, global unity among nations, nonviolence, rejection of extremism, nuclear disarmament, elimination of weapon profiteering, eradication of poverty, economic equity, service to humanity, universal human rights, international religious freedom, and democracy.

IN THE HOUSE OF REPRESENTATIVES

OCTOBER 12, 2018

Mr. KING of New York (for himself, Ms. SPEIER, Mr. PALLONE, Mr. McGOVERN, Mr. ROSKAM, Mr. POE of Texas, Mr. AGUILAR, Mr. RASKIN, Mrs. TORRES, Mr. McCAUL, and Mr. CONNOLLY) submitted the following resolution; which was referred to the Committee on Foreign Affairs

---

RESOLUTION

Welcoming His Holiness, Hadhrat Mirza Masroor Ahmad, the worldwide spiritual head of the Ahmadiyya Muslim Community, to the United States, including Pennsylvania, Maryland, Texas, Virginia, and Washington, DC, and recognizing his commitment to world peace, absolute justice, global unity among nations, nonviolence, rejection of extremism, nuclear disarmament, elimination of weapon profiteering, eradication of poverty, economic equity, service to humanity, universal human rights, international religious freedom, and democracy.

2

Whereas, from October 15, 2018, to November 5, 2018, His Holiness, Hadhrat Mirza Masroor Ahmad, the worldwide spiritual head of the Ahmadiyya Muslim Community, an international religious organization with millions of members across the globe, is making a historic visit to the United States, during which time he will inaugurate three new mosques: Baitul Aafiyat Mosque in Philadelphia, Pennsylvania, Baitus Samad Mosque in Baltimore, Maryland, and Masroor Mosque in Manassas, Virginia;

Whereas His Holiness was elected to become fifth Khalifa to Hadhrat Mirza Ghulam Ahmad, founder of the Ahmadiyya Muslim Community, on April 22, 2003, a lifelong position;

Whereas His Holiness is a leading Muslim figure promoting peace, who in his sermons, lectures, books, and personal meetings has continually advocated the Ahmadiyya Muslim values of service to humanity, universal human rights, and a peaceful and just society;

Whereas the Ahmadiyya Muslim Community has suffered repeated severe hardships, institutionalized discrimination, persecution, and violence in several countries in the world, including Pakistan, Indonesia, and Algeria;

Whereas, on May 28, 2010, 86 Ahmadi Muslims were killed in Lahore, Pakistan, when 2 mosques belonging to the Ahmadiyya Muslim Community were attacked by anti-Ahmadiyya terrorists and scores more have been killed in targeted attacks since then;

Whereas despite the continued sectarian persecution that Ahmadi Muslims are subjected to, His Holiness continues to forbid violence;

3

Whereas His Holiness has traveled globally to promote and facilitate service to humanity, meeting with Presidents, Prime Ministers, parliamentarians, and ambassadors of state;

Whereas His Holiness delivered the keynote address at a special bipartisan reception at the Rayburn House Office Building on Capitol Hill on June 27, 2012, "The Path to Peace: Just Relations Between Nations"; and

Whereas during his visit to the United States, His Holiness will meet thousands of American Muslims belonging to the Ahmadiyya Muslim Community in addition to significant United States Government leaders in order to strengthen relationships and find mutual means of establishing peace and justice for all people: Now, therefore, be it

1   *Resolved*, That the House of Representatives—

2   (1) welcomes His Holiness, Hadhrat Mirza

3   Masroor Ahmad, to Pennsylvania, Maryland, Texas,

4   Virginia, and Washington, DC;

5   (2) commends the tireless efforts of His Holi-

6   ness toward promoting a pathway to achieve indi-

7   vidual and global peace, as well as individual and

8   global justice;

9   (3) commends His Holiness for courageously

10   and unequivocally condemning extremism and terror

11   in all its forms; and

12   (4) commends His Holiness for his perseverance

13   in counseling all Ahmadi Muslims to eschew any

4

1   form of violence, even in the face of severe persecu-

2   tion.

○

SALUTATIONS

Salutations are recited out of respect when mentioning the names of Prophets and holy personages. These salutations have been abbreviated and inserted into the text where applicable. Readers are urged to recite the full salutations for the following abbreviations:

sas   *Sallallaahu 'alaihi wa sallam,* meaning 'May peace and blessings of Allah be upon him', is written after the name of the Holy Prophet Muhammad[sas].

as   *Alaihis-salaam,* meaning 'May peace be on him', is written after the names of Prophets other than the Holy Prophet Muhammad[sas].

GLOSSARY

Ahmadiyya Muslim Jama'at The Community of Muslims who have accepted the claims of Hazrat Mirza Ghulam Ahmad [as] of Qadian as the Promised Messiah and Mahdi. The Community was established by Hazrat Mirza Ghulam Ahmad [as] in 1889, and is now under the leadership of his Fifth *Khalifah*—Hazrat Mirza Masroor Ahmad (may Allah be his Helper). The Community is also known as **Jama'at-e-Ahmadiyya**. A member of the Community is called an **Ahmadi Muslim** or simply an **Ahmadi.**

Al-Imam al-Mahdi The title given to the Promised Reformer by the Holy Prophet Muhammad [sas]; it means the guided leader.

Aameen A term said after a prayer meaning, 'May Allah make it so.'

Assalaamo alaikum wa Rahmatullaahe wa Barakaatohu Traditional Islamic greeting, meaning, peace be on you, and the mercy of Allah and His blessings.

Hazrat A term of respect used for a person of established righteousness and piety; lit. 'His/Her Holiness.'

Holy Prophet[sas] A term used exclusively for the Founder of Islam, Hazrat Muhammad, may peace and blessings of Allah be upon him.

Holy Qur'an The Book sent by Allah for the guidance of mankind. It was revealed word by word to the Holy Prophet Muhammad [sas] over a period of twenty-three years.

Khalifah Successor. A Khalifah of Allah is a term used for a Prophet. Khalifah of a Prophet refers to his Successor who continues his mission.

Khalifatul-Masih A term used by the Ahmadiyya Muslim Jama'at to denote the Successors of the Promised Messiah[as].

Khilaafat The literal meaning of the term is successorship.

Mahdi The literal translation of this word is 'the guided one'. This is the title given by the Holy Prophet Muhammad[sas] to the awaited Reformer of the Latter Days.

Ta'awwuz Means seeking protection. The Arabic words are: *A'oozu Billaahi minash-Shaitaanir-Rajeem*, meaning: 'I seek refuge with Allah from Satan the Accursed.'

Tashahhud Means declaration. The Arabic words are: *Ash'hadu Allaa Ilaaha Illallaahu Wa Ash'hadu*

Anna Muhammadan Abduhu Wa Rasooluh, meaning: 'I bear witness that there is none worthy of worship except Allah; and I bear witness that Muhammad is His Servant and His Messenger.'

Bismillaah The Arabic words are *Bismillaahir-Rahmaanir-Raheem*, meaning, 'In the name of Allah, the Gracious, the Merciful.'

The Promised Messiah This term refers to the Founder of the Ahmadiyya Muslim Jama'at, Hazrat Mirza Ghulam Ahmad[as] of Qadian. He claimed that he had been sent by Allah in accordance with the prophecies of the Holy Prophet Muhammad[sas] about the coming of *al-Imam al-Mahdi* (the Guided Leader) and Messiah.